Back to Westphalia? The West's Waning Enthusiasm for Humanitarian Intervention

David Carlton

March 2010

About the Author

David Carlton is Professorial Research Fellow at the Global Policy Institute of the London Metropolitan University. Until his retirement in 2005 he was Senior Lecturer in International Studies at the University of Warwick. He is author of the following books: *MacDonald versus Henderson: The Foreign Policy of the Second Labour Government, 1929-1931* (Macmillan, London, and Humanities Press, New York, 1970); *Anthony Eden: A Biography* (Allen Lane, London, and Indiana University Press, Bloomington, 1981); *Britain and the Suez Crisis* (Blackwell, Oxford and New York, 1988); *Churchill and the Soviet Union* (Manchester University Press, Manchester and New York, 2000); *The West's Road to 9/11: Resisting, Appeasing and Encouraging Terrorism Since 1970* (Palgrave Macmillan, Basingstoke and New York, 2005); and (with David Thomas and Anne Etienne) *Theatre Censorship: From Walpole to Wilson* (Oxford University Press, Oxford and New York, 2008). He is also co-editor of 21 further volumes; and contributor to such academic journals as *Political Science Quarterly*; *The Historical Journal*; *Journal of Contemporary History*; *The Journal of Imperial and Commonwealth History*; and *Policy Review*.

Back to Westphalia? The West's Waning Enthusiasm for Humanitarian Intervention

The Background: Westphalian Norms

1618-1648 saw the Thirty Years War, a period of extreme anarchy during which state boundaries were generally not respected in Europe. At its end the Peace of Westphalia set in motion a process that produced new, widely-agreed ground rules for conduct of relations among sovereign states – and these so-called Westphalian norms form the basis for the mainstream rules and for much 'international law' down to the present. The two norms most relevant are that sovereign states are assumed, at least ideally, to have a monopoly on the use of politically-motivated armed violence; and that sovereign states are normally expected to respect the integrity of one another's frontiers and to avoid intervening with armed force in one another's internal affairs. These are of course extremely conservative norms. But they broadly underpinned the Covenant of the League of Nations (1919) and the Charter of the United Nations (UN) (1945) – even though the latter did contain some clauses concerning human rights. Yet at the extreme the only logical alternatives to this conservative rulebook may be either world government or universal anarchy. Any other intermediate positions may be difficult to define to the satisfaction of a majority of international actors and even more difficult to uphold in practice. In particular, we must ask whether humanitarian intervention by sovereign states, however ostensibly high-minded in motivation, into the affairs of others can be justified given the risk that a belief in predictable order in relations among all sovereign states will thereby be jeopardised; and whether, in the wake of 9/11 and with an increasingly plausible threat that Weapons of Mass Destruction could soon fall into the hands of terrorists, there can be 'good' terrorists with causes sufficiently just that the norm concerning the monopoly on organised violence belonging to sovereign states can be allowed to be systematically challenged without running the risk that eventually something approaching total anarchy will be the most likely result.

Challenges to Westphalian Norms from King Louis XIV to the Fall of the Berlin Wall

There have been of course over the centuries many unambiguous challenges to the Westphalian norms. For example

- There have been numerous cases of international expansionist acts of aggression by sovereign states from King Louis XIV to Adolf Hitler/Josef Stalin and beyond. Usually, however, the states concerned were sooner or later checked by a combination of other states. Often but not invariably they gave back some or all of their gains (an exception being, for example, the fact that Kaliningrad, formerly Königsberg, remains today firmly part of Russia notwithstanding its long history as a German-speaking Hanseatic city). But, perhaps most importantly, those concerned sooner or later returned at least rhetorically to the Westphalian fold.

- France supported international revolution between 1792 ('The Edict of Fraternity') and 1815 (the Fall of Napoleon). Incidentally, Great Britain went to war with Revolutionary France early in 1793 because of French insistence on supporting revolutionary elements in Holland and thus interfering in that country's internal affairs. The fact that France chose to become a republic and executed King Louis XVI together with numerous aristocrats was considered, on the other hand, to be a domestic matter and hence was not used by Prime Minister William Pitt the Younger as a justification for war.[1] This Westphalian approach, turned into a quasi-doctrine by Foreign Secretary Viscount Castlereagh in his celebrated State Paper of 5 May 1820, has since been followed with almost dogged consistency by Great Britain in its relations with other European powers – until the advent of the Government of Tony Blair which broke with tradition in choosing to attack Serbia (or Yugoslavia as it preferred to be known) because of its ill-treatment of its Kosovan minority. It is true of course that William Gladstone also disagreed with the Westphalian approach but he never actually went to war with another European power to promote humanitarian objectives, though from the Opposition benches he openly approved of Russia's intervention in the Ottoman Empire to assist the Bulgarian victims of atrocities and later also called in vain for armed intervention to assist the Armenians. Gladstone strongly disapproved, as Blair did later, of Otto von Bismarck, the German Chancellor, who at the Congress of Berlin in 1878 told the delegates: 'We are not here to consider the happiness of the Bulgarians but to secure the peace of Europe.' Earlier Bismarck had conceded to the Russians that 'as Christians we ought to have sympathy with suffering humanity everywhere and especially for suffering Christians in foreign lands' even though this sympathy did not oblige him to risk 'Germany's power, her peace and her European relations'.[2]

• In the era after the defeat of Napoleonic France in 1815 counter-revolutionary military intervention was from time to time carried out by the Holy Allies (Austria, Russia and Prussia), inspired by Count Metternich and Tsar Alexander the First, into countries they thought were threatened by internal revolutionary movements.[3] This was a kind of humanitarian intervention as seen through their eyes that was also at the same time a kind of counter-terrorism. This was unusual in that friends of counter-terrorism and friends of humanitarian intervention are seldom in practice on the same side in conflict situations.

- The Soviet Union in Stalin's time actively sent arms, money and instructions to member parties of the Communist International, thereby, for example, helping to bring down Germany's Weimar Republic in 1933 (a strategy, dictated by Stalin, against the advice of most leading German Communists, that had some unintended consequences!)

- The Soviet Union and various allies intervened in Czechoslovakia in 1968 in order to maintain Communism inside a fraternal state (the Doctrine of Limited Sovereignty for countries in the Socialist Camp or the Leonid Brezhnev Doctrine). Perhaps this should be seen in hindsight as intended to be a kind of humanitarian military intervention! Certainly admirers of Brezhnev (at one time said to approach two hundred million people in the countries of the Warsaw Pact not to mention friends in the West like the late Jack Jones, head of the million-strong British Transport and General Workers Union) may wish to argue such a case. For presumably in their eyes all the people of Czechoslovakia, joining together in stormy and prolonged applause, were spared for two complete decades from having to suffer under the horrors of the capitalism that today disfigures their tragic lives; the sad transformation being of course the fault of Mikhail Gorbachev, who in 1989 capriciously declined to act similarly to Brezhnev and thus returned Moscow, after its extremely lengthy digression into the wilder shores of radical international experimentation and glorious abnormality, to the traditional path of ghastly Westphalian orthodoxy.

- The United States gave active military support during the 1980s to 'terrorists' in Nicaragua (the Contras) and in Afghanistan (the Mujaheddin) despite maintaining diplomatic relations with the governments they hoped to see overthrown. No American Administration has since seen fit to apologise for this misconduct judged by Westphalian standards – even though all have expressed outrage at the failure of successive Iranian Governments to apologise for the actions of those who similarly broke the rigid rules of diplomacy at the time of the US Embassy occupation between 1979 and 1981.

- Above all, there is the undeniable fact that many of today's sovereign states were born as a result of 'terrorists' or 'freedom fighters' overthrowing 'foreign', 'colonialist', 'reactionary', 'fascist' or 'racist' rulers who had been broadly acknowledged at the time as sovereign under Westphalian norms. George Washington, Giuseppe Garibaldi, Giuseppe Mazzini, as well as too many heroes of twentieth century anti-imperialist struggles to list here, spring readily to mind. It is thus hardly surprising that many of today's leaders, while intermittently supportive of the rhetoric of counter-terrorism, hesitate to dwell on aspects of their own country's history that appear to point in a different direction.

The 1990s: A Decade of Optimism about Human Rights and of Liberal Challenges to Westphalian Norms

The end of the Cold War was immediately followed by unusual harmony and a good deal of ideological agreement among Great Powers. Hopes grew that henceforth the international system could be managed successfully and that nuclear and much other weaponry could be effectively controlled, reduced and eventually rendered completely obsolete. We even saw the publication by Francis Fukuyama of a book entitled *The End of History* that foresaw a liberal democratic future for the entire planet once a small minority of anti-democratic hold-outs had disappeared and once various pockets of anarchy and poverty had been tackled.[4] An excellent start for the optimists was made in 1991 when the UN Security Council, no longer hobbled by frequently-used vetoes, encouraged a US-led coalition of more than forty states (including some Arab ones) to use armed force to evict Saddam Hussein's Iraq from Kuwait, which had been brutally invaded in the previous year. Then came an UN-approved US intervention in Somalia to try to bring effective government to a country plagued with warlordism. The Americans soon pulled out but most opinion-formers in the world applauded the idealism involved and few pointed out that intervening in the internal affairs of Somalia was arguably contrary to Westphalian norms. Then came more widespread anarchy and warlordism in Rwanda with approaching a million people eventually being killed. On this occasion there was no UN-approved international intervention on a serious scale if only because no Great Power, not even the United States, was prepared to do the 'heavy lifting' in so inhospitable an arena. But the consciences of President Bill Clinton and many other Americans were apparently deeply troubled by what they saw on CNN and they determined to do better when fighting and even anarchy intensified throughout the Balkans.

Most Great Powers, though increasingly not Russia and China, decided to approve of the breakup of Yugoslavia, even though Westphalian norms favoured maintenance of existing international borders in the absence of the consent of the recognised central government. Eventually reluctant acquiescence from Belgrade was effectively wrung by NATO for the emergence as sovereign states of Slovenia, Croatia, the Federal Republic of Macedonia and even Bosnia (after brutal US arm-twisting at Dayton). But Belgrade drew the line at the possible loss of Kosovo (which was widely seen by Serbs as historically part of Serbia even though a large majority of those residing in the province were by the 1990s Albanian Moslems seeking to secede). Westphalian norms and 'international law' seemed and still seem to favour Belgrade – as both Russia and China insist. But, a less-than-enthusiastic Clinton, strongly pressurised by the anti-Westphalian humanitarian idealist Blair (note his famous speech in Chicago on 24 April 1999 to which we shall return) and US Secretary of State Madeleine Albright (who was a migrant from Eastern Europe), decided to lead NATO in an armed attack, without any authorisation from the UN Security Council, on Serbia in 1999 with no narrow self-interest (such as protecting oil supplies) being involved. But high-minded though the NATO leaders clearly were, they thus nevertheless placed themselves on the same side as the 'terrorists' of the Kosovan Liberation Army (KLA). Their view was of course that as many innocent Kosovan Moslems were being subjected to genocidal attacks by Serb armed forces, whether or not provoked by KLA violence, the normal rules concerning non-intervention in internal affairs of sovereign states and avoidance of association with 'terrorists' should be flouted. Their supporters claimed that while ignoring the thrust of Westphalia, the League of Nations Covenant and the UN Charter, they were nevertheless building on a more modern and better tradition that arguably began just after the end of the Second World War when all the Great Powers (including even Stalin's Soviet Union!) signed up to the Universal Declaration of Human Rights. They thus claimed and still claim that the attack was 'legitimate' even if it was not 'legal'. On the other hand, they have tended to have less to say about the threat that 'terrorism' already constituted during the 1990s, preferring to see 9/11 as the beginning of a completely new chapter.

Many academics in the International Relations discipline were also naturally greatly exercised by developments concerning humanitarian intervention and most, it seems, were broadly supportive. Yet at the same time many could see that changes in the way the international system was managed could go too far and too fast. For example, Nicholas J. Wheeler of the

University of Wales, Aberystwyth, expressed his reservations at the beginning of 2001:

> The challenge facing those who represent humanity at the UN is to engage in a genuine dialogue over the substantive rules that should determine a legitimate humanitarian intervention. A key issue here concerns persuading Member States, especially the permanent members, that there should be restrictions on the exercise of the veto in the Security Council. There is an emergent norm in the society of states that governments that commit crimes against humanity within their borders should forfeit the protection afforded them by the rules of sovereignty and non-intervention. However, few governments are prepared to countenance humanitarian intervention in the absence of express Security Council authorization. Trespassing with this core Charter principle conjures up the anarchical image of the floodgates being opened to intervention leading to a collapse of the structure of global order. This argument is most strongly voiced by those who fear that the doctrine of humanitarian intervention is a new form of western imperialism, but it strikes a chord with the governments that are generally sympathetic to the claim that the balance between sovereignty and human rights should be shifted in favour of the latter.[5]

In fact 1999, we can now see with hindsight, marked the high-water mark of the humanitarian intervention movement in the West that followed the end of the Cold War. It is noteworthy, for example, that no front-bench British politician in either the Commons or the Lords condemned the NATO assault on Serbia – with the sole exception of Lord Skidelsky (who was immediately dismissed as a Conservative spokesman for making known his dissent). But to some extent Clinton and Blair failed even in 1999. For Russia sent troops to assist Belgrade and appeared ready to confront NATO if full independence for Kosovo (as Albright had effectively promised) was promoted. The result was an uneasy compromise whereby Kosovo remained legally part of Serbia but was administered by an international body known as Operation Allied Force pending further negotiations among UN Security Council members – a process that is in a certain legal sense still uncompleted. For our purposes, however, it seems fair to conclude that the Western Powers in 1999 had seen fit to move away from two central Westphalian norms, namely non-intervention in internal affairs and the belief that sovereign states should have a monopoly on politically-motivated armed violence. But the shift was not destined to be built upon in the new century. For the tragic events of 11 September 2001 brought the West substantially back into line with more traditional thinking now apparently backed in broad substance in both Moscow and Beijing.

The New Century: the Impact of the 'Global War on Terrorism' on the Prospects for Humanitarian Intervention

Immediately after 9/11 the Great Powers on the Security Council came together in united horror at what had occurred. And, like almost all other states, they condemned what was seen as a systemic attack on not just the United States but in effect on sovereign states *per se* by non-state actors. There was also widespread disgust at the role Mullah Omar's Afghanistan saw fit to play as a protector of Osama bin Laden and al-Qaeda. So when a US-led coalition invaded Afghanistan and toppled the Taliban regime the UN Security Council was supportive and the 'Global War on Terrorism' had wide international support. None was more enthusiastic at the time than Vladimir Putin's Russia. For now the United States and indeed NATO as a whole felt bound to soft-pedal their carping criticisms of Russian counter-terrorist measures in Chechnya and largely to fall silent on their arguments in favour of humanitarian intervention into Serbia's internal affairs. Suddenly, then, Westphalian norms were back.

Moreover, despite the acute differences that have arisen among Great Powers over the US-led invasion of Iraq, these norms have not so far been centrally challenged in the new century. True, the invasion of Iraq was not explicitly authorised by the UN Security Council. But neither President George Bush the Younger nor even the agile Blair have so far argued that the *principal* reason for overturning Saddam Hussein was as a result of his brutal ill-treatment of his own people or his genocidal attacks on Iraqi Kurds. And no mention is ever made by these or any other Western leaders of the fact that Saddam Hussein's regime, like all its predecessors going back as far as the break-up of the Ottoman Empire, ran an apartheid-like system under which the minority Sunni Arab community left the larger Shia community with negligible representation in the leading organs of the state, including the armed forces. Rather the central US and NATO grievance seems to have derived from the fact that Saddam Hussein had failed to meet obligations to cooperate fully with UN arms inspectors in the aftermath of his illegal attack on the sovereign state of Kuwait – a thoroughly justified concern that was merely heightened among some US policy-makers by intelligence reports, many supplied in 'sexed-up' form by London, that Iraq might or did already possess Weapons of Mass Destruction. True, Blair may have had other priorities harking back to Kosovo and even to Gladstone, as is suggested by a close reading of his seminal Chicago speech of 1999. In this speech he condemned the unfeeling inhumanity of Bismarck (Gladstone's *bête noire*); and he pointedly linked the names of Slobodan Milosevic and Saddam Hussein ('Many of our problems have been caused by two dangerous and ruthless men – Saddam Hussein and Slobodan Milosevic. Both have been prepared to wage vicious campaigns against sections of their own community. As a result of these destructive policies both have brought calamities to their own peoples.').[6] Moreover, some American religious fundamentalists (and/or so-called neo-cons) undoubtedly wanted to engage in 'nation-building' and 'democracy promotion'. But the key country was the United States not Great Britain, almost all of whose somewhat conceited leaders needed, then as now, to be reminded that they represented only one per cent of the world's population and needed also to be reminded (as they crushingly were in 2003 by US Secretary of Defense Donald

Rumsfeld) that the United States stood in no absolute need of any British military support whatsoever in Iraq. And the key US players in 2003 were not the idealists but Bush the Younger, Rumsfeld and Vice-President Richard Cheney who appear to have been at best only fleetingly troubled by what would happen to the people of Iraq in the probable chaos that would ensue after Saddam Hussein's fall and the disbandment of the army that was thought to be unhealthily loyal to him. In short, the US decision to merely topple rather than positively replace Saddam Hussein was driven more by Westphalian than by humanitarian reasoning; and because of Iraq's unpurged delinquency in invading Kuwait it was arguably much more in line with 'international law' than the NATO attack on Serbia four years earlier had been. This absence of serious US concern with humanitarian aims was confirmed at least initially by what came to be known as the 'Rummy-Light' approach, that was an at best half-hearted commitment of US troops clearly intended for early withdrawal. True, a degree of 'mission creep' later developed, particularly after Robert Gates succeeded Rumsfeld, and this may to some extent have been influenced by humanitarian idealists on the Religious Right of the United States. But certainly at the outset the Iraq mission was centrally driven by more traditional thinking (though Bush the Younger may have had an undeclared personal grievance against Saddam Hussein for the part he was suspected of playing in trying to have George Bush the Elder assassinated on a visit to Kuwait on 14 April 1993).

If a case can be made that US supporters of Westphalia lost some ground with the passage of time in Iraq, it is not on the other hand easy to claim that this trend was accompanied by a revival of a more general appetite in the West or in the wider international community for humanitarian intervention. On the contrary, few seem now to expect the Great Powers, either collectively or unilaterally, to intervene militarily for humanitarian reasons in the Darfur province of Sudan; or in Myanmar (Burma); or in Zimbabwe; or in Sri Lanka; or in Somalia. This is not to say that Western policy with respect to counter-terrorism and humanitarian military intervention is now wholly consistent. But it seems to this observer that, with new leaders in the White House and in Number 10 Downing Street, there is now a bias in favour rather than against Westphalian norms; and that international humanitarian concerns now count for much less than during the Clinton Presidency and the Blair Premiership. All the same, it may be worth listing a few of the contradictory aspects of recent and current policy so that the extent of the survival of the spirit of 1999 in the face of 9/11 can be considered:

- Despite their silence on Chechnya, most NATO states (though not quite all) continue to favour a full triumph for the KLA 'terrorists' over Serbia. And to a large extent this was achieved during the final year of the Presidency of Bush the Younger. At the same time, on the other hand, diplomatic recognition of the new regime in Pristina is still being withheld by in particular Russia, which seems, however, to have mainly responded, disappointingly for Westphalian purists, by recognising breakaway statelets from Georgia rather than by giving any material assistance to Serbia. A consolation for Westphalian purists is that so far none of the illegal breakaway European statelets, whether sponsored by Russia or by the West, have been able to overcome Security Council vetoes blocking their entry into the UN.

• The United States has long vacillated in its attitude to Pakistan even though it is aware that many elements within that country sponsor 'terrorists' in Afghanistan and in Kashmir.

• Western Powers are reluctant to face up to their past willingness to sponsor or give comfort to 'terrorists' such as the Mujaheddin and the Contras during the 1980s and to the KLA in the 1990s. And few prominent Americans seem eager to debate whether or not Washington was a 'terrorist'.

• The United States has ignored Venezuelan requests for the extradition of an alleged bomber of a Cuban airline.

• The International Criminal Court continues to function. But its practical importance has scarcely been seen as enhanced since 9/11. For example, there appears to be no appetite on the part of any Great Power to try to deliver Israeli leaders for trial on war crimes charges following Justice Richard Goldstone's UN report on the Gaza conflict. Likewise, the arrest and temporary detention in London of Chile's General Augusto Pinochet at the behest of a Spanish judge for crimes allegedly committed within Pinochet's own country turned out to be an isolated event and not the beginning of a revolutionary dash towards a global system of justice (or possibly a global system of very uneven justice indeed involving delinquent leaders of weak states being treated very differently from delinquent leaders of strong states) that would have dealt a crushing blow to Westphalian assumptions.

- The rise of China as a leading actor in the international system has accelerated since 9/11. And since it has a Communist Government supposedly committed to international revolutionary Marxist-Leninist ideals one might have expected that this would be an ominous development for adherents of Westphalia. And in the long run this may yet prove to be the case. But so far 21st Century China has been a strong supporter of national sovereignty in the international system and not at all reluctant to strike commercial deals with functioning regimes no matter how odious their domestic records (whether from a humanitarian or from a Marxist-Leninist standpoint) may be. For example, Sudan appears to have no firmer friend in the international system than China.

- For its part the West seems unclear whether armed rebels in Darfur and also in other areas of Sudan are to be treated as 'terrorists', as 'freedom fighters' or as victims of government brutality. Some US spokespersons have even accused Khartoum of genocide although others pointedly avoid doing this.

• Western statesmen seem reluctant to acknowledge that when they protest volubly about human rights abuses in this or that country they encourage victims to respond with 'terrorist' campaigns in the hope of provoking further repression that could trigger a humanitarian military intervention from outside.

All of these issues, and more, mean that the interface between so-called humanitarian intervention and so-called counter-terrorism will continue to provoke heated debate as to the broad direction in which we are moving. But the present writer is persuaded that no leading state has any enthusiasm for a systematic pursuit of humanitarian intervention that could lead to a significant loss of blood and treasure let alone a heightened risk of Great Power confrontations. Above all, Barack Obama, though his Presidency is obviously still a work in progress, shows no sign of wishing to return to the heady days of the Clinton-Blair promotion of regime change apparently for no better reason than that it was 'morally right'. Those who doubt this should study with care Blair's speech at Chicago on 24 April 1999 and compare it with those of Obama during his first year in the White House, and particularly with that given at Cairo University in June 2009 and at Oslo, on the occasion of his acceptance of the Nobel Peace Prize, in December 2009.

Blair: A Unique Contribution to the Practice of Statesmanship?

Blair in his Chicago speech presumably saw himself as the reincarnation of Gladstone (although his mindset also contained echoes of Anthony Eden of which he was probably completely unaware). He declared:

> While we meet here in Chicago this evening, unspeakable things are happening in Europe. Awful crimes that we never thought we would see again have reappeared – ethnic cleansing, systematic rape, mass murder. I want to speak to you this evening about events in Kosovo. But I want to put these events in a wider context....No one in the West who has seen what is happening in Kosovo can doubt that NATO's military action is justified. Bismarck famously said that the Balkans were not worth the bones of one Pomeranian Grenadier. Anyone who has seen the tear-stained faces of the hundreds of thousands of refugees streaming across the border, heard their heart-rending tales of cruelty or contemplated the unknown fates of those left behind, knows that Bismarck was wrong. This is a just war based not on territorial ambitions but on values. We cannot let the evil of ethnic cleansing stand. We must not rest until it is reversed. We have learned twice before in this century that appeasement does not work. If we let an evil dictator range unchallenged we will have to spill infinitely more blood and treasure to stop him later.[7]

Almost exactly ten years later, on 23 April 2009, an unrepentant Blair returned to Chicago to review his earlier speech and since he was by then out of office it can be safely assumed that his words were not drafted for him by temporary or permanent civil servants (which could have been the case with at least some of his earlier offering).[8] He declared: 'Here is where I remain adamantly in the same spot, metaphorically as well as actually.' He went on in a passage that borders on sounding narcissistic and that reminds us that, in contrast to his successor Gordon Brown, he has never had a reputation as a particularly keen student of history:

> In that speech, I set out what I described as a doctrine of international community that sought to justify intervention, including if necessary military intervention, not only when a nation's interests are directly engaged; but also when there exists a humanitarian crisis or gross oppression of a civilian population. The statesmanship that went before regarded politics as a Bismarck or Machiavelli regarded it. It's all a power play, a matter not of right and wrong, but who's on our side, and our side defined by our interests, not our values. The notion of humanitarian intervention was the meddling of the unwise, untutored and inexperienced.[9]

What is particularly striking and even breathtaking is that he appeared to believe 'the statesmanship that went before' could be dismissed in a few glib sentences and that he, on the other hand, represented a greatly superior moral brand of statesmanship based on 'values'. He appears, in short, to believe that all his predecessors in the practice of statesmanship had had no 'values' whatsoever just because they were not the same as his. Such a view can be easily contested. Let us consider, to take one prominent example, the case of President Woodrow Wilson. Towards the end of the First World War he grappled long and hard with the issue of reshaping the international system, and not just with the aim of serving narrow US interests. This was made abundantly clear in his famous Fourteen Points laid down on 8 January 1918 and in the Four Principles presented to a joint session of Congress on 11 February 1918. He had in contemplation a League of Nations to maintain peace among states in the post-war world in a high-minded system that came to be known as Collective Security. But he was also initially tempted to ask the leading members of the League not only to discipline states that crossed frontiers in acts of aggression but in addition to make provision for the promotion of self-determination of peoples, which, he declared to Congress was 'an imperative principle of action which statesmen will henceforth ignore at their peril'[10] – a sentiment that would presumably have been applauded by both Blair and the KLA in 1999. But Robert Lansing, Wilson's Secretary of State, saw that prevention of armed aggression by sovereign states and the promotion of self-determination for minorities could only lead to intolerable tensions and doom the League of Nations to having an essentially incoherent set of missions. As Lansing put it:

> Fixity of national boundaries and of national allegiance, and of political stability would disappear if this principle [of self-determination] was uniformly applied. Impelled by new social conditions, by economic interest, by racial prejudices,

and by various forces, which affect society, change and uncertainty would result from an attempt to follow the principle in every case to which it is possible to apply it.[11]

Eventually Wilson reluctantly fell in with Lansing's advice and the League of Nations Covenant as adopted contained nothing that authorised collective interference in the internal affairs of sovereign states. But it is truly difficult to argue that Wilson in decisively shaping the creation of the League, whatever its merits and demerits, had not all the same represented some 'values' that went far beyond the promotion of US self-interest.

There have been plenty of British statesmen, too, during the last century and before whose approach to international affairs has been far from narrowly nationalistic. A recent example would be Margaret Thatcher, whose response to Argentina's seizure of the Falkland Islands was surely driven by far more than a calculated assessment of the economic stake her country had in the South Atlantic or even electoral advantage. She clearly felt an obligation to rescue the settler community from occupation or eviction. And, as she made known to President Ronald Reagan, she was acutely conscious of the precedent being created by Argentina for other possible acts of 'unprovoked aggression' throughout the world. As she wrote in her memoirs: 'We were defending our honour as a nation, and principles of fundamental importance to the whole world – above all, that aggression should never succeed and that international law should prevail over the use of force.'[12] And Thatcher was not alone among Blair's predecessors in having believed in combining serving the national interest with the wider well-being of the international system – usually presented to the country as enlightened self-interest. Indeed, it has been cogently argued by Correlli Barnett, in a series of four books, collectively described by him as his 'Pride and Fall' sequence, that in the case of the British the high-minded enlightenment has too often dwarfed the self-interest.[13] He attributed this to the fact that many British statesmen have been heavily influenced by religiously-inspired exhortations to pursue 'All that is Noble and Good' (the title of the second chapter of the first book in his sequence). In the case of the 'toffs' (mainly Conservative) the public school ethos memorably preached by Dr. Thomas Arnold of Rugby School has been dominant, whereas on the Left the puritan influence deriving from non-conformity has much responsibility. (Thatcher was unusual among Prime Ministers in being from the Right but not being born a 'toff' – but she too had a religious background, her father being a Methodist lay preacher.) Barnett focused on the character and outlook of various interwar leaders prominent in foreign policy-making and assembled many telling quotations relating to them. Here are just a few:

- Of Ramsay MacDonald (Labour Prime Minister and Foreign Secretary, 1924; Labour Prime Minister, 1929-1931; and National Labour Prime Minister, 1931-1935; a Presbyterian): '[He] really was persuaded that "our true nationality is mankind"...he really did believe that men were naturally good, that they could be brought into line though they looked like horses at a starting gate for ever facing opposite ways and savaging each other....In short and his own words [*sic*] he held that we were eternally moving in a great surge towards righteousness.'

- Of Sir John Simon (National Liberal Foreign Secretary, 1931-1935; son of a Congregationalist Minister): '[He] spent a successful life on earth without learning its ways, for he was unworldly though the reverse of other-worldly....'

- Of Arthur Henderson (Labour Foreign Secretary, 1929-1931; and briefly Leader of the Opposition; a Methodist lay preacher): '[He] had the faith of a child in noble dreams, and an unshakeable confidence in the ultimate goodness of a world that might look evil, but yet had something in it of the divine.'

- Of Lord Halifax (National Conservative Foreign Secretary, 1938-1940; a high-church Anglican): '[He possessed] a sweet and Christian nature.'[14]

None of these interwar statesmen, and most others among their contemporaries, lacked values in the sense that Blair thinks Bismarck and Machiavelli did. On the other hand, they were not all in agreement with one another as to how British foreign policy should be conducted in practice – though all paid at least lip-service to showing fidelity to the League of Nations. The difficulty was that they were spoiled for choice when it came to being 'Noble and Good'. Some saw the League of Nations as a valuable forum in which to try to settle international disputes whereas others wanted in addition to use it to maintain order in the international system by threatening the use of sanctions (economic and/or military) against aggressors, with some among the latter favouring action only if Great Britain had plenty of allies (so-called *Collective* Security). But there were other distracting proposals. For example, there was a widespread belief that disarmament was a key to promoting peace (though there were divisions among unilateralists and multilateralists; and divisions among those who favoured prioritised action on naval disarmament and those who wanted *all* armaments to be targeted simultaneously, a difference of emphasis symbolised by MacDonald playing a leading role at the London Naval Conference of 1930 and Henderson concentrating on the inconclusive World Disarmament Conference which he chaired during the early 1930s). And there were those who thought that the League of Nations needed to be supplemented by a European collective security arrangement (with the Draft Treaty for Mutual Assistance (1923), the Geneva Protocol (1924) and the Locarno Treaties (1925) attracting competing followers). Another perspective was that the United States (which did not join the League of Nations despite the best efforts of Wilson) needed to be drawn into the management of the international system – leading to the emergence of enthusiasts for the Kellogg-Briand Pact of 1928. It is thus difficult to see in all this activity, however ultimately futile it turned out to be, any basis for Blair's dismissal of his predecessors as lacking in values.

Maybe the episode from the interwar years that most relates to Blair's preoccupations in his Chicago speech arose during 1935-1936 when Italy successfully conquered Abyssinia/Ethiopia. Italy announced that it was engaged on a 'Civilising Mission'. And certainly Abyssinia, one of very few African countries that was not a European colony, had many deplorable characteristics such as having a medieval monarchy, chronic tribal warlordism, and, above all, a system of slavery nearly a century after the slave trade had been stamped out and many decades after the institution had been abolished in both the United States and Russia. True, as a *de facto* independent sovereign state, it had been admitted to the League of Nations in 1923 but a number of countries had objected, including Great Britain, Australia, Norway and Sweden, 'on the grounds that the Government in Addis Ababa appeared to exercise only a precarious control over large areas of the country and had made little effort to stamp out slavery or control the widespread arms traffic that existed there'.[15] Would it, then, be safe to assume that Blair, if he knows anything about these events, would be sympathetic to the Italian cause seemingly so similar in character to that of NATO in attacking Serbia in 1999? Actually no. For Italy had another less noble reason for invading Abyssinia, notably that it wanted revenge for defeat in 1896, when at the Battle of Adowa the Abyssinians had defeated its attempt in the context of the Scramble for Africa to obtain another colony. Moreover, Italy in 1935 was ruled by a Fascist dictator who was seen by many high-minded British statesmen as 'dangerous and ruthless' – just as Milosevic and Saddam Hussein seemed to Blair. So would Blair not logically have wanted Great Britain and any allies it could recruit to seek to topple the unsatisfactory regimes in *both* Rome and Addis Ababa? But no British leaders at the time favoured such an approach in the case of *either* Italy *or* Abyssinia. Instead, they focused on the fact that Italy had broken the League Covenant by crossing another sovereign state's frontier. As a result the British Government led the way in securing League condemnation of Italy and the institution of selective economic sanctions against it. These proved unsuccessful in bringing Mussolini to heel. So British statesmen then had to decide whether to escalate the economic sanctions and thereby run the risk of having to go to war on behalf of Abyssinia. Chancellor of the Exchequer Neville Chamberlain, some will think surprisingly, favoured imposing an oil sanction but his colleagues would not accept this in the face of the unwillingness of other leading League states, and especially France, to go further down the road of alienating Rome at a time when it was widely thought that Italy might yet be drawn into playing a role in checking the emerging ambitions of Nazi Germany. And so sanctions collapsed and Italy succeeded in conquering Abyssinia. Opinions will differ as to when British statesmen went wrong in this crisis. Some will say that they were too idealistic from the outset and others will say that they were not idealistic enough. But who will say, apart perhaps from followers of Blair, that they showed themselves to possess no high-minded values at all because they were not obsessed with achieving regime change in either Rome or Addis Ababa or both?

Some of the same moral dilemmas presented themselves in 1938 when Hitler (another 'dangerous and ruthless' man) sought to promote self-determination for the three million ethnic Germans living in multi-ethnic Czechoslovakia. Over the heads of the sovereign Government in Prague and hence in defiance of Westphalian norms, Chamberlain, supported by France, rather than face war for the sanctity of frontiers, arranged at the Munich Conference for the transfer of the Sudetenland to Germany – initially to widespread plaudits throughout the world (with even President Franklin Roosevelt sending the British Prime Minister a congratulatory telegram). As A. J. P. Taylor wrote in 1961:

> It was a triumph for all that was best and most enlightened in British life; a triumph for those who had courageously denounced the harshness and short-sightedness of Versailles. [H. N.] Brailsford, the leading Socialist authority on international affairs, wrote in 1920 of the peace settlement: 'The worst offence was the subjection of over three million Germans to Czech rule.' This was the offence redressed at Munch. Idealists could claim that British policy had been tardy and hesitant. In 1938 it atoned for these failings. With skill and persistence, Chamberlain brought first the French, and then the Czechs, to follow the moral line.[16]

There is no doubt that most Sudetens welcomed the transfer. For in that period at least ethnic identity appears to have trumped living in a democracy as a first priority for many Europeans – witness the fact that in 1934 ninety per cent of Saarlanders in an internationally-supervised plebiscite chose Nazi Germany over the French Republic. Yet can we safely take it that Blair, on the admittedly rather large assumption that he is familiar with the relevant history, retrospectively applauds Chamberlain's choice of 'humanitarian intervention' on behalf of the Sudeten people over strict adherence to the then prevailing norms of 'international law'? Actually it would seem not. For, as we have seen, in his Chicago speech in 1999, presumably with Munich in mind, he offered the strikingly unoriginal view that 'we have learned twice before this century that appeasement does not work'.

Of course Hitler was a 'dangerous and ruthless' man whose persecution of the Jews may seem from the perspective of our own day to be self-evidently of absolutely central importance – completely dwarfing any case there may have been for urging self-determination for the Sudetens. But few people in September 1938 seem to have seen it that way. Even those who favoured war with Germany, for example Winston Churchill, criticised the Munich agreement mainly on geopolitical not humanitarian grounds – essentially they held that Germany was bidding for mastery of Europe and had to be stopped at the earliest opportunity. In short, theirs was a Westphalian position. And later in 1938 an event occurred which tends to confirm that humanitarian concerns about anti-Semitism were of entirely secondary importance to the leading Western statesman of the day. This was when Nazi activists, with the approval of the German Government, carried out a pogrom, known as *Kristallnacht*, against Jews still living in Germany – attacking synagogues and shops. But there was no suggestion from any serious quarter in any country that armed humanitarian intervention should be undertaken. In short, much as Blair's followers may wish it had been otherwise, resistance to racial persecution was not central to the coming of the Second World War. Indeed, Great Britain and France saw fit in March 1939 to give fateful security guarantees to Poland notwithstanding the fact that it was not a democracy and that its own Jews were frequently victims of racial discrimination. Thus when war over Poland broke out in the following September it was primarily a war about Westphalian norms. And, although this widened into a World War in the following years, it largely remained so. In short, the Holocaust came to loom large in the thinking of statesmen and peoples alike only in the post-war era. But most of the statesmen of the West during the Second World War had been fighting for high-minded values all the same.

If, then, Blair really thinks that the statesmanship of all or even most of his predecessors was essentially no different from that of Bismarck ('Blood and Iron') and Machiavelli, then maybe critics can and indeed should make the argument that he belongs among 'the unwise, untutored and inexperienced'. Certainly it is beyond doubt that he was unusually inexperienced when he first entered Number 10 Downing Street. For he came to the highest office with no previous record of service in any governmental capacity – something that had applied to MacDonald in 1924 but to no other British Prime Minister. He was of course not to blame for this and nor were those who selected him as Leader of the Labour Party in 1994 on the death of John Smith. The fault, if any, lay with those whose actions and inactions had caused one of the two major British 'Parties of State' to languish, divided and demoralised, in the political wilderness for no less than 18 years, during which period all of James Callaghan's senior ministers had retired or died or deserted the Labour Party, leaving only a team of relative neophytes to face the Conservatives in the General Election of 1997. But while the charge that Blair was 'inexperienced' at the time of his Chicago speech in 1999 seems reasonable enough, it does not necessarily follow that he was 'unwise' and 'untutored'. And the fact that in 2009 he claimed to hold the same broad view as in 1999, after serving as Prime Minister for ten years, has to be taken into account. All the same, the present writer does think that there is more than a whiff of naivety about his original Chicago speech. And he thinks that this is further illustrated by the inadequacy of one of the few qualifying passages to be found therein. It reads:

> Looking around the world there are many regimes that are undemocratic and engage in barbarous acts. If we wanted to right every wrong that we see in the modern world then we would do little else than intervene in the affairs of other countries. We would not be able to cope.[17]

How superficially reasonable this recognition of the problem of potential 'mission overload' sounds; and how it echoes, probably unconsciously, the US isolationist critique of Wilsonian hopes of bringing collective security to interstate relations via the League of Nations as being tantamount to promising 'to wage perpetual war for perpetual peace'. But Blair's apparent wish to engage in such righting of wrongs as Great Britain and any allies could 'cope' with actually made little sense if he did not attempt to meet, which he did not, the argument that other Great Powers, not necessarily sympathetic to his own values, might equally insist on intervening in the domestic affairs of other states, again of course only no doubt to the extent that they judged that they could 'cope'. And then there is the vital issue of 'uneven justice'. What would be the fate of such benighted countries as had leaders prepared to engage in 'barbarous acts' but where no external states at all, whether approved or disapproved by Blair, would be willing to intervene for fear of not being able to 'cope'? In this context Rwanda and the Central African Republic spring to the present writer's mind. But did they spring to Blair's mind? We may never know. All the same he gave every impression whether in 1999 or 2009 of having nothing to say about the problem of 'uneven justice' or about the possibility that a Great Power like China or Russia might take 'international law' into its own hands for purposes not welcome in London (and as Russia actually did in 2008 with respect to Georgia). And his silence on these matters means that he indeed risked being seen in the long run as 'unwise' and 'untutored'.

True, Blair did attempt to spell out in his speeches in Chicago in both 1999 and 2009 (see Appendices I and II) how he saw the West's place in world affairs and which tests he thought should apply before his country should become involved in a humanitarian war. But his approach seemed to be based on little more than traditional Roman Catholic just war doctrines. And he failed to address concerns about 'uneven justice', about how other Great Powers might react to unilateral acts by NATO states and about what role the UN Security Council might be expected to play. At all events, there has been little by way of consistent attempts by Blair to apply his own tests. For example, his stated desire to see UN reform appears tokenist, given that he had apparently blocked a Foreign Office bid to insert a more substantial test relating to the UN in his first Chicago speech and given that, according to Oliver Daddow, 'impatience with the nature and pace of UN reform was one of Blair's bugbears'.[18] And of course when it came to the invasion of Iraq in 2003 Blair's approach seemed to some, particularly with hindsight, to be almost entirely devoid of nuance and even at its heart pitifully simplistic. For example, Blair's predecessor Sir John Major told listeners to the BBC on 2 January 2010:

> The suspicion arises that this was more about regime change than it was about weapons of mass destruction. There are many bad men around the world who run countries and we don't topple them, and indeed in earlier years we had actually supported Saddam Hussein when he was fighting Iran. The argument that someone is a bad man is an

inadequate argument for war and certainly an inadequate and unacceptable argument for regime change.[19]

Obama's First Year: A Return to Westphalia?

Obama is the first Democrat to occupy the White House since Clinton pioneered, with Blair, uninvited military intervention in sovereign states for exclusively humanitarian purposes. Yet during his first year in office Obama, notwithstanding his appointment of Clinton's wife Hillary as Secretary of State, has been extremely sparing in making any references to his predecessor, let alone to his distinctive contribution to the conduct of US foreign relations. Indeed, the suspicion must be that he identifies more with the ultra-Westphalian Bush the Elder than with any other recent President. Here I intend briefly to examine three of Obama's principal orations during 2009 to illustrate this point: his Inaugural (20 January); his address at Cairo University (4 June); and his acceptance speech in Oslo following his award of the Nobel Peace Prize (9 December).

Obama's Inaugural was surprisingly light on foreign policy and contained little that was memorable (in contrast, for example, to that of President John F. Kennedy in 1961). But he did offer a few interesting words that could be characterised as the reverse of a ringing declaration:

> They [earlier generations] understood that our power alone cannot protect us, nor does it allow us to do as we please. Instead they knew that our power grows through its prudent use. Our security emanates from the justness of our cause;

the force of our example; the tempering qualities of humility and restraint....

We'll begin to responsibly leave Iraq to its people, and forge a hard-earned peace in Afghanistan....[20]

Obama was obliged to say rather more than this in Cairo, as the entire speech was about US foreign policy, naturally with particular reference to the Middle East. His remarks about the region were well-received at least among governments and opinion-formers in the region who were hostile to Iran. He naturally benefited from simply not being Bush the Younger and maybe also from being the first non-white US President. But his speech did not mark a great turning point in the history of the Middle East and, above all, was not followed by any breakthrough in the deadlock between Israel and the Palestinians. Nor did he say much about humanitarian intervention that would have given pleasure to Blair and his supporters. They cannot have drawn much comfort, for example, from these reflections:

> I know there has been controversy about the promotion of democracy in recent years, and much of this controversy is connected with the war in Iraq. So let me be clear: No system of government can or should be imposed by one nation on any other.

Many uplifting words about democracy followed but readers will judge for themselves whether they constitute any indication that the United States is now any more than lukewarm about the approach presented in Blair's

Chicago speech (see Appendix III). Maybe more telling is a single sentence to be found near the beginning of his speech: 'So America will defend itself, respectful of the sovereignty of nations and the rule of law.'[21] To this writer it seems as conservative a sentiment as any Westphalian could hope to hear.

Another essentially cautious and measured speech was offered at the Nobel Peace Prize ceremony. But here he recognised that his audience would want at least some recognition of developments in the workings of the international system since the end of the Cold War. So he candidly acknowledged that 'wars between nations have increasingly given way to wars within nations'. He continued: 'The resurgence of ethnic or sectarian conflicts; the growth of secessionist movements, insurgencies and failed states – all these things have increasingly trapped civilians in unending chaos.' But he offered only somewhat vague indications about what the US response to these developments should be (and for some of these see Appendix IV). On the other hand, one somewhat imprecise nod in Clinton's direction came when he said: 'The service and sacrifice of our men and women in uniform has promoted peace and prosperity from Germany to Korea, and enabled democracy to take hold in places like the Balkans.' And another such nod came when he declared: 'I believe that force can be justified on humanitarian grounds, as it was in the Balkans, or in other places that have been scarred by war....But in a world in which threats are more diffuse, and missions more complex, America cannot act alone.'[22]

It was at the Nobel Prize ceremony, however, that Obama came closest to facing up quite squarely to what Blair represented and tacitly rejecting it. He began the relevant passage in an apparently Blairite way: 'The promotion of human rights cannot be about exhortation alone.' But instead of raising the possibility of at times using armed force, as many in his audience may have expected, he chose instead to say limply that 'at times, it [exhortation] must be coupled with painstaking diplomacy'. He continued: 'I know that engagement with repressive regimes lacks the satisfying purity of indignation. But I also know that sanctions without outreach – condemnation without discussion – can carry forward only a crippling status quo.'[23] It is surely inconceivable that Blair would have uttered such 'defeatist' words once he had delivered his seminal Chicago speech. In short, it would appear that the humanitarian interventionist hour is over and that, in the West at least, Westphalian norms are once again back in fashion.[24]

Appendices

Appendix I: Extract from Speech by Blair in Chicago, 24 April 1999

So how do we decide when and whether to intervene? I think we need to bear in mind five major considerations.

First, are we sure of our case? War is an imperfect instrument for righting humanitarian distress; but armed force is sometimes the only means of dealing with dictators. Second, have we exhausted all diplomatic options? We should always give peace every chance, as we have done in the case of Kosovo. Third, on the basis of a practical assessment of the situation, are there military operations we can sensibly and prudently undertake? Fourth, are we prepared for the long term? In the past we talked too much of exit strategies. But having made a commitment we cannot simply walk away once the fight is over; better to stay with moderate numbers of troops than return for repeat performances with large numbers. And finally do we have national interests involved? The mass expulsion of ethnic Albanians from Kosovo demanded the notice of the rest of the world. But it does make a difference that this is taking place in such a combustible part of Europe.

Appendix II: Extracts from Speech by Blair in Chicago, 23 April 2009

Many... described the speech [of 24 April 1999] as hopelessly idealistic, dangerous even. And, probably, in the light of events since then, some would feel vindicated. As for me, I am older, better educated by the events that shaped my premiership, but I still believe that those who oppress and brutalise their citizens are better put out of power than kept in it....

We are standing up for what is right. The body of ideas that has given us this liberty, to speak and think as we wish, that allows us to vote in and vote out our rulers, that provides a rule of law on which we can rely, and a political space infinitely more transparent than anything that went before; that body isn't decaying. It is in the prime of life. It is the future. And though the extremists that confront us have their new adherents, we have ours too, nations democratic for the first time, people tasting freedom and liking it.

And that is why we should not revert to the foreign policy of years gone by, of the world weary, the supposedly sensible practitioners of caution and expediency, who think they see the world for what it is, without the illusions of the idealist who sees what it could be.

We should remember what such expediency led us to, what such caution produced....

...was it practical to let Pakistan develop as it did in the last thirty years, without asking what effect the madrassas would have on a generation educated in them? Or wise to employ the Taliban to drive the Russians out of Afghanistan? Or to ask Saddam to halt Iran? Was it really experienced statesmanship that let thousands upon thousands die in Bosnia before we intervened or turned our face from the genocide in Rwanda? Or to form alliances with any regime, however bad, because they solve 'today' without asking whether they will imperil 'tomorrow'? That isn't statesmanship. It is just politics practiced for the most comfort and the least disturbance in the present moment. I never thought such politics very sensible or practical. I think it even less so now. We live in the era of interdependence; the idea that if we let a problem fester, it will be contained within its boundaries no longer applies. That is why leaving Africa to the ravages of famine, conflict and disease is not just immoral but immature in its political understanding. Their problems will become ours.

Appendix III: Extracts from Speech by Obama in Cairo, 4 June 2009

Let me address the issue of Iraq. Unlike Afghanistan, Iraq was a war of choice that provoked strong differences in my country and around the world. Although I believe that the Iraqi people are ultimately better off without the tyranny of Saddam Hussein, I also believe that events in Iraq have reminded America of the need to use diplomacy and build international consensus to resolve our problems whenever possible....

...No system of government can or should be imposed by one nation upon any other. That does not lessen my commitment, however, to governments that reflect the will of the people. Each nation gives life to this principle in its own way, grounded in the traditions of its own people. America does not presume to know what is best for everyone, just as we would not presume to pick the outcome of a peaceful election. But I do have an unyielding belief that all people yearn for certain things: the ability to speak your mind and have a say in how you are governed; confidence in the rule of law and the equal administration of justice; government that is transparent and doesn't steal from the people; the freedom to live as you choose. These are not just American ideas; they are human rights. And that is why we will support them everywhere.

Now there is no straight line to realize this promise. But this much is clear: Governments that protect these rights are ultimately more stable, successful and secure. Suppressing ideas never succeeds in making them go away. America respects the right of all peaceful and law-abiding voices to be heard around the world, even if we disagree with them. And we will welcome all elected, peaceful governments – provided they govern with respect for all their people.

Appendix IV: Extracts from Speech by Obama in Oslo, 9 December 2009

We must begin by acknowledging the hard truth: We will not eradicate violent conduct in our lifetimes. There will be times when nations – acting individually or in concert – will find the use of force not only necessary but morally justified.

...I believe that all nations – strong and weak alike – must adhere to standards that govern the use of force. I – like any head of state – reserve the right to act unilaterally if necessary to defend my nation. Nevertheless, I am convinced that adhering to standards, international standards, strengthen those who do, and isolates and weakens those who don't.

The world rallied around America after the 9/11 attacks, and continues to support our efforts in Afghanistan, because of the horror of those senseless attacks and the recognized principle of self-defense. Likewise, the world recognized the need to confront Saddam Hussein when he invaded Kuwait – a consensus that sent a clear message to all about the cost of aggression. Furthermore, ...no nation...can insist that others follow the rules of the road if we refuse to follow them ourselves. For when we don't, our actions appear arbitrary and undercut the legitimacy of future interventions, no matter how justified. And this becomes particularly important when the purpose of military action extends beyond self-defense or the defense of one nation against an aggressor. More and more, we all confront difficult questions about how to prevent slaughter of civilians by their own government, or to stop a civil war whose violence and suffering can engulf an entire region.

Notes

1   William Hague, *William Pitt the Younger* (HarperCollins, London, 2004), chs 16-17.

2   A. J. P. Taylor, *Bismarck: The Man and the Statesman* (Hamish Hamilton, London, 1955), pp. 167, 177. See also W. N. Medlicott, *The Congress of Berlin and After: A Diplomatic History of the Near Eastern Settlement, 1878-1880* (Methuen, London, 1938); and W. N. Medlicott, *Bismarck, Gladstone and the Concert of Europe* (Athlone Press, London, 1956).

3   See various essays in Alan Sked (ed.), *Europe's Balance of Power, 1815-1848* (Macmillan, London and Basingstoke, 1979).

4   Francis Fukuyama, *The End of History and the Last Man* (Penguin, London, 1992).

5   Nicholas J. Wheeler, 'Humanitarian Intervention after Kosovo: Emergent Norm, Moral Duty or the Coming Anarchy?', *International Affairs*, vol. 77, no. 1, January 2001, pp. 127-8.

6   http://keeptonyblairforpm.worldpress.com/blair-speech-transcripts-from1997-2000/#chicago Accessed 1 January 2010.

7   Ibid.

8   It has even been claimed, however, that much of the 1999 speech was actually drafted by someone from outside the Westminster/Whitehall nexus, namely Professor Lawrence Freedman, Professor of War Studies at King's College, London. Freedman himself is the source. Oliver Daddow, '"Tony's War"? Blair, Kosovo and the Interventionist Impulse in British Foreign Policy', *International Affairs*, vol. 85, no.3, May 2009, p. 556.

9   http://tonyblairoffice.org/2009/04/tony-blair-speech-to-chicago-c.html Accessed 1 January 2010.

10 On Wilson see John A. Thompson, 'Wilsonianism: The Dynamics of a Conflicted Concept', *International Affairs*, vol. 86, no. 1, January 2010, pp. 27-47. See also David Carlton, 'Boundary Change and Ethnic Separation in South-Eastern Europe, 1919-1999: The Role of the Great Powers', in John Rex and and Gurharpal Singh (eds), *Governance in Multicultural Societies*, (Ashgate, Aldershot, Hampshire, and Burlington, Vermont, 2004), pp. 103-4.

11 Robert Lansing, *The Peace Negotiations* (Houghton Mifflin, Cambridge, Massachusetts, 1921), pp. 96-7.

12 Margaret Thatcher, *The Downing Street Years* (HarperCollins, London, 1993), pp. 173, 230-1.

13 Correlli Barnett, *The Collapse of British Power* (Eyre Methuen, London, 1972); *idem, The Audit of War: The Illusion and Reality of Britain as a Great Nation* (Macmillan, London, 1986); *idem, The Lost Victory: British Dreams, British Illusions, 1945-1950* (Macmillan, London, 1986); and *idem, The Verdict of Peace: Britain Between Her Yesterday and the Future* (Macmillan, London, 2001).

14 Barnett, *The Collapse of British Power*, pp. 64-5. Barnett's sources were: (for MacDonald and Simon) Lord Vansittart, *The Mist Procession* (Hutchinson, London, 1958), pp. 373-4, 427; (for Henderson) Mary Agnes Hamilton, *Arthur Henderson* (Heinemann, London, 1938), p. 446; and (for Halifax) Harold Macmillan, *Winds of Change* (Macmillan, London, 1966), p. 531.

15 A. J. Barker, *The Civilizing Mission: The Italo-Ethiopian War, 1935-6* (Cassell, London, 1968), p. 26.

16 A. J. P. Taylor, *The Origins of the Second World War* (Hamish Hamilton, London, 1961), p. 235.

17 See text of speech cited in Note 9 above.

18 Daddow, '"Tony's War"?', pp. 556-7.

19 http://news.bbc.co.uk/IHI/uk/84337422.stm Accessed 15 January 2010.

20 www.cnn.com/2009/Politics/01/21/obama Accessed 15 January 2010.

21 http:// www.whitehouse.gov/the-press-office/remarks-president-at-cairo-university-6-4-09/ Accessed 1 January 2010.

22 http:// www.whitehouse.gov/the-press-office/remarks-president-acceptance-nobel-peaceprize. Accessed 1 January 2010.

23 Ibid.

24 An earlier and briefer version of this study was presented to the 21st Winter Course of the International School on Disarmament and Research on Conflicts at Andalo, Italy, in January 2008.